Louis Weber, CEO
Publications International, Ltd.
7373 North Cicero Avenue
Lincolnwood, Illinois 60712

Permission is never granted for commercial purposes.

ISBN-13: 978-1-4127-1324-5
ISBN-10: 1-4127-1324-2

Manufactured in China.

8 7 6 5 4 3 2 1

IF DOGS COULD TALK

TONGUES UNLEASHED!

Written by Joel Zadak

Publications International, Ltd.

No, because if I "drop it" you're just going to throw it again.

A third-string
pitcher is so
underappreciated.
Have you seen my
curveball?

I <u>do</u> love you. I'm just not ready to announce it to the world.

Wanna go outside? Let's go outside. Can we go outside? We should go outside. Have you been outside?

I won't tell
if you
won't tell.

Blondes do
have more
fun.

Right now I'm doing your typical puppy jobs, but what I really want is to direct.

I have to walk
her twice a day.

My backside smiles so much,
my mouth doesn't have to.

I'll hide out here until they put the two-year-old to bed.

I may not be able to run
anymore, but I'm wise
enough to appreciate the
days when I could.

I know I messed up, but people really need to realize they can't have nice things <u>and</u> a puppy.

They
always say
they'll only
be a
minute.

I like the idea of a sandwich,
I've just never had the patience
to actually make one.

Can we do a picture with just the two of us? My ribs are killing me.

We have to go home now.

I need to call my broker.

I ran. I got the ball.
I brought it back.
Now what?

I wasn't worried until he started calling me his little McNugget.

Yeah, I ate the
boy's homework.
That's what I
love to do, eat
boys' homework.

Why do you guys think Mom's so happy all of a sudden?

No squirrel may pass.
I am the Squirrel Master.

Uh, you guys might want to sleep downstairs tonight.

Pssst . . .
do you want to
know a secret?

I'm all ears.

Drop it. Drop it. Drop it.
Drop it. Come on, drop it.

This is torture. Someone call
the ASPCA.

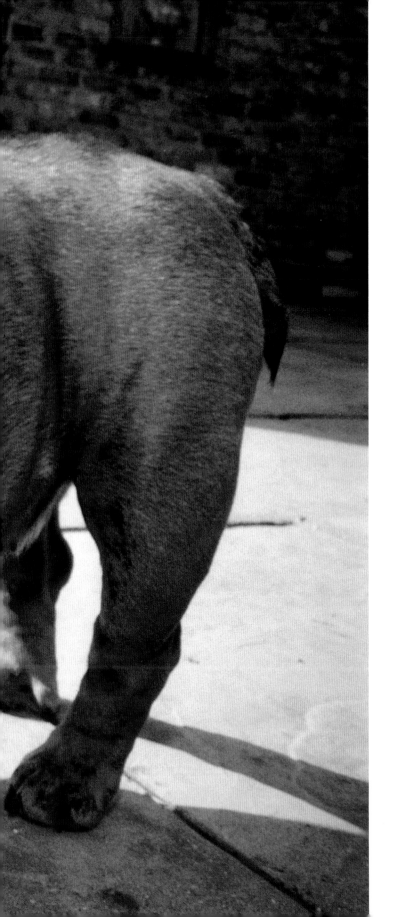

You're definitely
picking the
wrong day to
mess with me.

Come to think of it, I probably should have opted for the money-back guarantee.

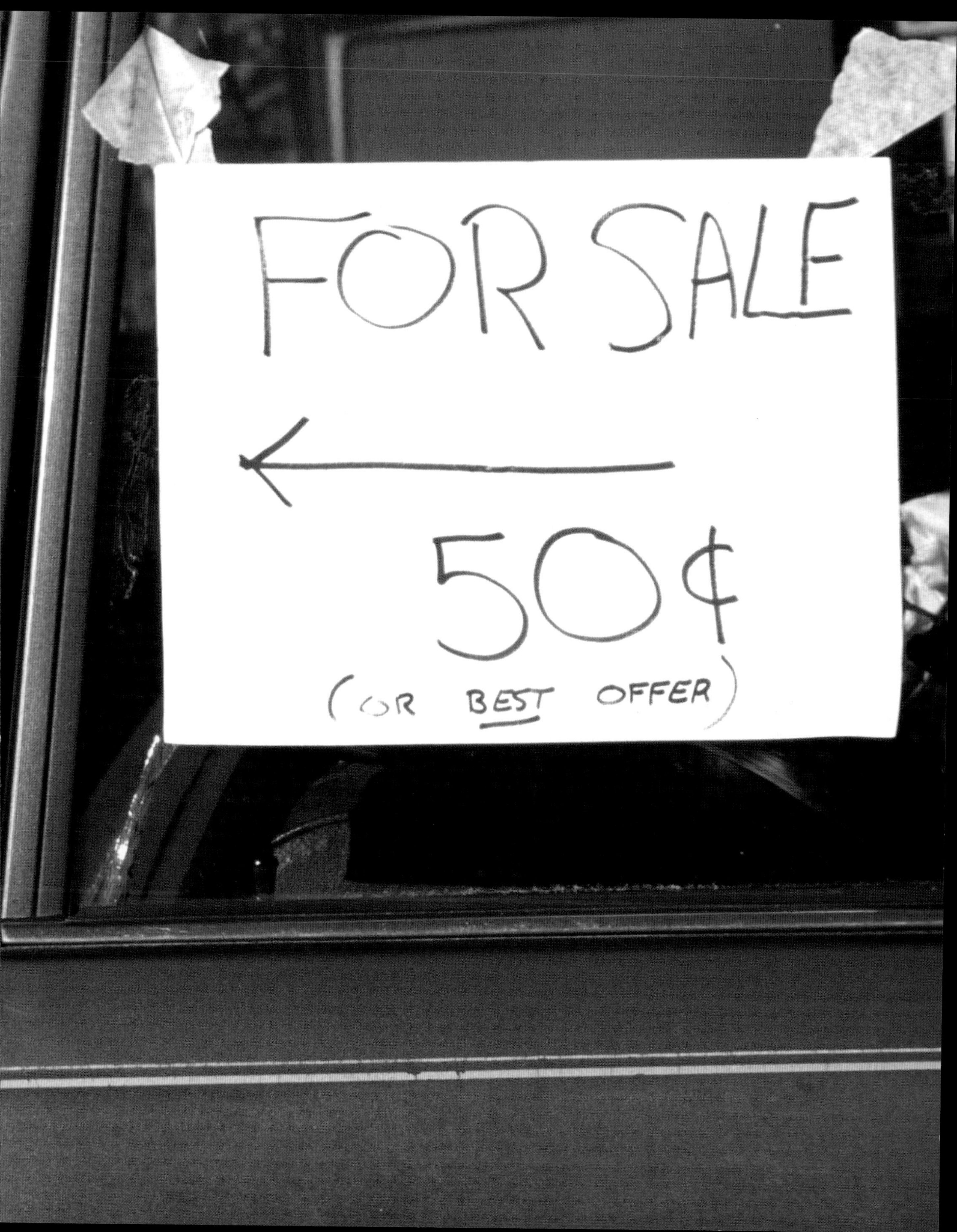
FOR SALE
50¢
(OR BEST OFFER)

Come on now,

big girls
don't cry.

I can't believe we
have the same mother.

What obedience class? I was trained on the streets.

Sometimes I feel I'm a Jack Russell trapped in a bulldog's body. But then that goes away and I just sleep the rest of the day.

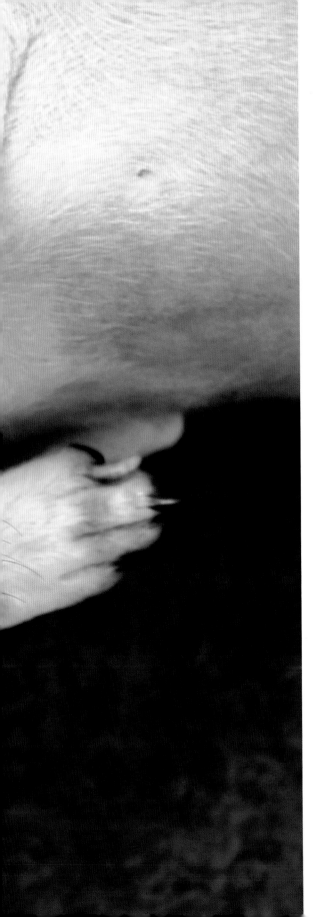

Don't look! I
haven't put on
my makeup yet.

I got my master's degree
from Barker College
and my Ph.D. from DePaw.

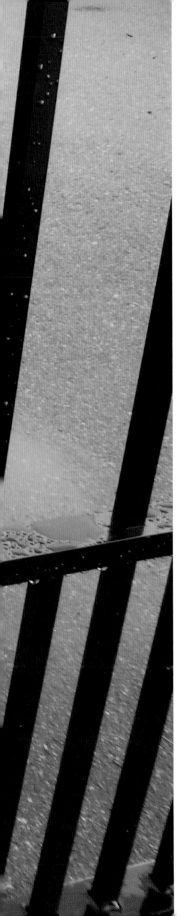

I only chewed up
one shoe. This seems like
a pretty steep sentence
for one lousy shoe!

Just <u>leave</u> me alone,

would ya?

Just wanted to make sure you don't need any help. I'd be happy to help...really...just let me help!

I'm not tired. It's the ball
that needs a rest.

This is where I nap. I sleep in a king-size bed with satin sheets and fluffy pillows.

I'm telling you,
I'm not wearing the leash
in this family!

I thought I told her to upgrade me to first class!

What, me come there?
Why can't you come here
just this once?

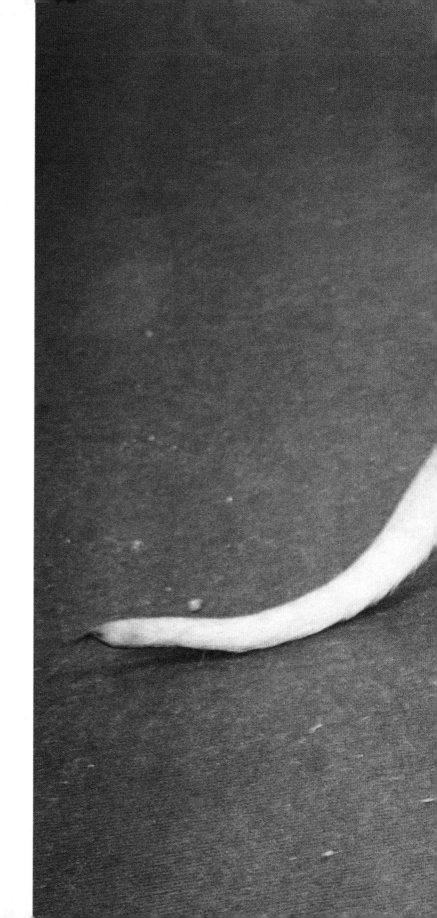

The end.

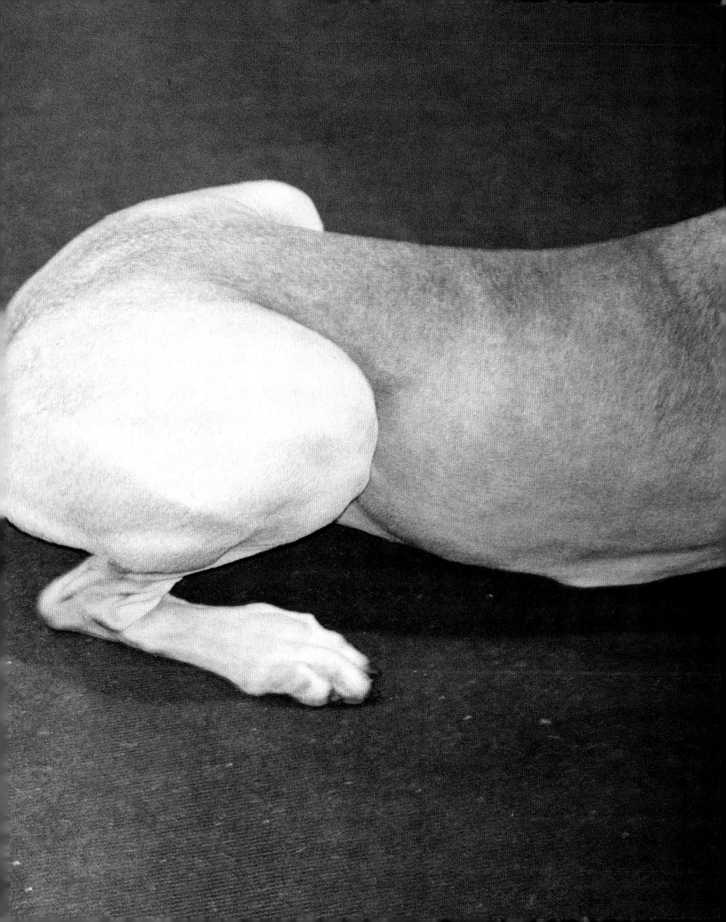